12/0

THE HOUSTON TEXANS, THE INDIANAPOLIS COLTS, THE JACKSONVILLE JAGUARS, AND THE TENNESSEE TITANS

INSIDE THE NFL

AFC SOUTH: The Houston Texans, The Indianapolis Colts, The Jacksonville Jaguars, and The Tennessee Titans

Published in the United States of America by The Child's World®
P.O. Box 326 • Chanhassen, MN 55317-0326 • 800-599-READ • www.childsworld.com

Editorial Directions, Inc.: E. Russell Primm, Editorial Director and Line Editor; Elizabeth K. Martin, Assistant Editor; Olivia Nellums, Editorial Assistant; Susan Hindman, Copy Editor; Susan Ashley, Proofreader; Kevin Cunningham, Fact Checker; Tim Griffin/IndexServ, Indexer; James Buckley Jr., Photo Researcher and Selector

The Child's World®: Mary Berendes, Publishing Director

Photos: All photographs by Sports Gallery/Al Messerschmidt except for: AP/Wide World: 1, 11, 26, 31, 32, 41, 42; Corbis: 16, 18.

LIBRARY OF CONGRESS CATALOGING-IN-PUBLICATION DATA
Buckley, James, 1963–
 The AFC South : the Houston Texans, the Indianapolis Colts, the Jacksonville Jaguars, and the Tennessee Titans / by James Buckley Jr.
      p. cm. – (The Child's World of sports. Inside the NFL)
Summary: Introduces the four teams that since 2002 are the American Football South Conference of the National Football League. Includes bibliographical references and index.
 ISBN 1-59296-026-X (Library Bound : alk. paper)
 1. National Football League–History–Juvenile literature. [1. National Football League–History. 2. Football–History.] I. Title. II. Series.
 GV955.5.N35B823 2003
 796.332'64'0973–dc21   2003004302

3 1559 00158 9918

TABLE OF CONTENTS

INTRODUCTION

In 2002, the National Football League (NFL) changed the way its teams are organized. The league moved from six divisions of four-to-six teams to eight divisions of four teams each. One of these new divisions was the AFC (American Football Conference) South. The four teams in this division remind us of an old saying often heard at weddings. Brides are supposed to wear "something old, something new, something borrowed, and something blue."

There are two "old" teams in this division and two very new ones. There are two teams that have been permanently "borrowed" from other cities by their current cities. And there are three teams that prominently feature blue in their uniforms.

Along with a scorecard, you need a map to keep track of the AFC South. The Tennessee Titans used to be the Houston Oilers. That old NFL city got a brand-new team, the Houston Texans. The Indianapolis Colts used to play in Baltimore. And the Jacksonville Jaguars put that small Florida city on the NFL map.

Though the teams all have colorful histories, they haven't been as successful as other divisions.

Only the Colts, when they played in Baltimore, have won an NFL championship (in 1970). However, the Titans and Jaguars have come close, and the Texans are just getting started, so give them some time!

The AFC South has some very good teams playing in it. They are all just hoping to walk down the aisle someday with the Super Bowl trophy. Here's an inside look at this interesting quartet of teams.

JACKSONVILLE JAGUARS

Year Founded: 1995

Home Stadium: ALLTEL Stadium

Year Stadium Opened: 1995

Team Colors: Teal, black, and gold

Tennessee and Jacksonville are AFC South rivals.

TENNESSEE TITANS

Year Founded: 1960

Home Stadium: Coliseum

Year Stadium Opened: 1999

Team Colors: Navy blue, red, and silver

CHAPTER ONE

THE HOUSTON TEXANS

Los Angeles's loss was Houston's gain. In late 1997, the NFL announced that it would expand by one to a total of 32 teams. The league also said it would be the last **expansion** team for quite some time. The cities of Los Angeles and Houston both put up great bids to earn that 32nd team. NFL owners carefully considered all the factors, while fans in both cities waited anxiously.

They were all used to having NFL football. Los Angeles had been home to the Rams from 1946 to 1994, when they moved to St. Louis. Houston had hosted the Oilers from 1960 to 1996, but then that team moved to Tennessee to become the Titans (see chapter 4). Both cities had NFL history on their side, and both cities had ownership groups with huge amounts of money. In the end, though, Houston promised to build a stadium, and that made the difference.

When Houston was announced as the winner of

the new team in 1997, the city erupted with cheers. They had missed pro football since the Oilers left. Now, new owner Bob McNair was ready to make Houston a pro football hotbed again. He had to spend a record $700 million for the privilege of doing this. And the city of Houston had to help him build a brand-new stadium for his new team.

The Texans' first game was the pre-season Hall of Fame Game in Canton, Ohio. They lost 34–17 to the New York Giants.

Reliant Stadium is the Texans' brand-new home.

Coach Dom Capers knows something about building a winner from scratch: He took the Panthers to the NFC title game in only their second season in 1996.

McNair and his **associates** got right to work. Their first employee was a veteran NFL talent scout named Charley Casserly. Casserly had been a key executive with the Washington Redskins when that team won several Super Bowls. Casserly spent the next year preparing all aspects of the team, from the uniforms to the training facilities. Finally, in

Businessman Robert McNair is the owner of the Texans.

January 2001, he hired Dom Capers to be the team's first head coach. By the end of 2001, the team had signed its first free agents and was preparing for its first NFL **draft** in April 2002.

Building a brand-new NFL team takes time and a lot of energy. New teams are given extra draft picks to help them stock their rosters. They are given a **budget** of money to sign free agents, too. Casserly and Capers chose some players who could help right away, and others they could spend time developing into stars.

Former Panthers coach Dom Capers led the Texans in their first season.

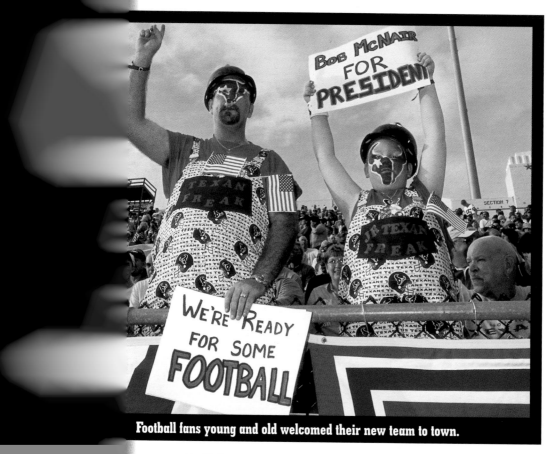

Football fans young and old welcomed their new team to town.

In February 2002, the team was allowed to choose from a limited number of players from other teams. The first player they chose was offensive tackle Tony Boselli. The former All-American had been a Pro Bowl player for Jacksonville for seven seasons. Other key players taken in this draft were cornerback Aaron Glenn and defensive tackle Gary Walker.

Aaron Glenn celebrates after intercepting a pass
in the Texans' first game.

Quarterback David Carr was the Texans' first draft pick.

In April, the NFL held its annual draft of college players. With the first overall pick in the draft, Houston chose quarterback David Carr from Fresno State. In the draft's seven rounds, they added 11 more players. Slowly, the building blocks of an NFL team were being assembled.

Nearly 100 players and more than a dozen coaches and staff met in July for the team's first training camp. NFL teams practice in the heat of summer to prepare for the coming season. For the Texans, it was more than just another series of practices, however. This camp would set the tone for their whole first season.

Capers emphasized defense, knowing that that skill can often be easier to master more quickly. If he could keep other teams from scoring too much, he might have just enough offense to win a few games. After several exhibition games, the team finally was ready to play its first regular-season game on September 8, 2002.

Reliant Stadium was filled with more than 69,000 fans, all eager to see the Texans defeat their in-state **rival,** the Dallas Cowboys. Carr came out smoking. He threw a 19-yard touchdown pass to tight end Billy Miller for the team's first touchdown. Capers's plan of playing tough defense paid off. Dallas quarterback Quincy Carter rarely had time to operate.

For the first time since 1961, an NFL expansion team won its very first game, as the Texans defeated the Cowboys 19–10.

It had been a hectic three years for McNair, Casserly, Capers, and company, but it had paid off. Of course, success is more than just one win, and

A good start: Carr shouts for joy after completing the
first touchdown pass in team history!

Houston struggled for much of its first season. But
if determination and good ol' Texas guts mean any-
thing, the Texans should put their brand on the
NFL very soon.

CHAPTER TWO

THE INDIANAPOLIS COLTS

The Colts are the only team in NFL history that could include a moving van in their logo. The team began play in 1947 in Miami, moved to Baltimore in 1948, and in 1984 moved to Indianapolis. The owner in 1984, Robert Irsay, didn't bother to tell anyone about the move. One snowy night, moving vans drove up to team headquarters, packed up, and left for Indianapolis. Just like that, the city of Baltimore lost its beloved NFL team.

The Colts began life in 1947 as the Miami Seahawks in the All-America Football Conference (AAFC). The AAFC was a short-lived rival to the NFL. In 1950, the Colts, Browns, and 49ers from the AAFC joined the NFL. After losing money, the team sat out the 1951 and 1952 seasons. A "new" Colts team began play in 1953. Over the next few years, coach Weeb Ewbank assembled some great players. They included quarterback Johnny Unitas, receiver Raymond Berry, tackle Jim Parker, and

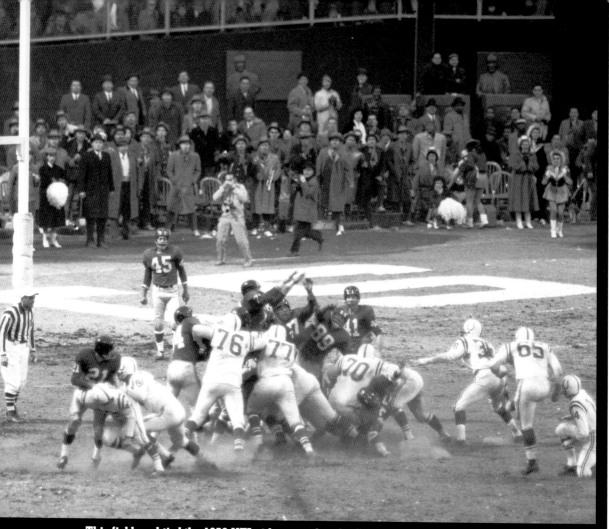

This field goal tied the 1958 NFL title game that the Colts later won in overtime.

defensive end Gino Marchetti. The team improved
gradually and made it all the way to the top of the
NFL in 1958.

The NFL Championship Game of 1958 is still
called "the greatest game ever played." The Colts
faced the New York Giants in Yankee Stadium in
one of the first title games ever broadcast on TV. A
huge audience saw a thrilling game. The Colts tied

it at 17–17 with a field goal in the final seconds. But this was a championship, and there had to be a winner. For the first time, **sudden-death overtime** would be used to decide the winner. The first team to score would win.

Unitas was superb. As a quarterback, he has had few equals in league history. He was an expert at moving his team quickly with little time left. In overtime, he used this technique to march down the field. Though they were close enough for an easy field goal, he chose to go for the touchdown. After completing a pass to the 1-yard line, Unitas handed off to Alan "The Horse" Ameche. He charged into the end zone, the Colts were champs, and the NFL entered a new, TV-filled **era.**

The Colts repeated as champs in 1959 but lost the title game in 1964. In 1968, packed with new stars that included running back Tom Matte and tight end John Mackey, the Colts put on a rare show. The team finished the regular season with only one loss. The defense tied a record by allowing only 144 points. After winning the NFL title easily, Baltimore faced the AFL champs, the New York Jets, in Super Bowl III. Though Baltimore was

Before joining the Colts in 1955, Johnny Unitas had played semipro football in Pennsylvania for six dollars a game.

How nervous was rookie Jim O'Brien before kicking the winning field goal in Super Bowl V? He tried to pick up a blade of grass to gauge the wind—but the game was played on artificial turf!

Johnny Unitas is regarded as perhaps the greatest quarterback of all time.

heavily **favored,** the Jets pulled off one of the greatest upsets in sports history. They defeated a team many consider one of the best ever, 16–7, in a game that made Jets quarterback Joe Namath a star.

Two years later, the Colts returned to Super Bowl V. This time, Baltimore emerged as champions when rookie kicker Jim O'Brien nailed a game-winning field goal with five seconds left.

The Colts returned to the playoffs three more times in the 1970s. Their stars

Bert Jones led the Colts in the 1970s

included running back Lydell Mitchell, who
became the team's first 1,000-yard runner in 1975.
Quarterback Bert Jones was among the NFL's best.
However, they didn't reach the big game, and the
team faded later in the decade.

In 1984, the team underwent its biggest
change. Though teams are supposed to alert the
league when they move, Robert Irsay didn't bother
with that detail. He worked out a deal to move the
Colts to Indianapolis. Then he headed west before
anyone knew what was going on. Baltimore fans,

When the regular
quarterbacks were
hurt in late 1965,
running back Tom
Matte took over. He
wore a plastic brace
on his wrist with a
list of plays to call!

Jim Harbaugh led the Colts in the
1995 AFC Championship Game.

In Indianapolis, the Colts have an indoor home: The RCA Dome.

who loved their team no matter how well it did, were devastated. Pro football didn't come back to "Charm City" until 1995, when the Cleveland Browns became the Baltimore Ravens.

In Indianapolis, the Colts moved to an indoor stadium now called the RCA Dome. The team's brightest moment was in 1995 when it came one play short of reaching another Super Bowl. They had earned a **wild-card** playoff berth and reached

In 1999, Edgerrin James led the NFL in rushing as a rookie with 1,553 yards. He was the first rookie to do so since Eric Dickerson in 1983.

Peyton Manning is
the son of former
NFL quarterback
Archie Manning,
who played for the
Saints, Oilers, and
Vikings in his
14-year career.

the AFC Championship Game. Led by quarterback Jim Harbaugh, the Colts fell to the Steelers 20–16. Harbaugh's long pass on the final play was nearly caught by a Colts receiver in the end zone.

Another quarterback has proved to be the latest success in Colts history. Peyton Manning was chosen by the team in the 1998 draft, and he quickly

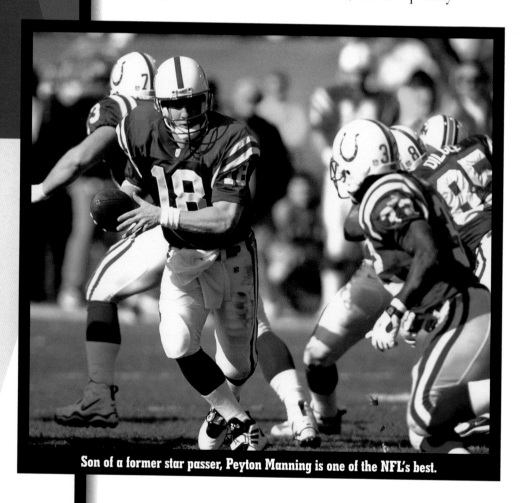

Son of a former star passer, Peyton Manning is one of the NFL's best.

became an elite pro passer. He set numerous rookie passing records in 1998 and then led the Colts to a division title in 1999. Manning has teamed with receiver Marvin Harrison and running back Edgerrin James to give the team one of the NFL's top offensive trios. These days, the Colts concentrate on moving the ball—not the entire team!

Marvin Harrison set an NFL record when he caught 143 passes in 2002. He easily surpassed Herman Moore's mark of 123 for the Lions in 1995.

Edgerrin James is always among league leaders in rushing yards.

CHAPTER THREE

THE JACKSONVILLE JAGUARS

Jacksonville is the second-smallest city to play host to an NFL team (behind Green Bay and the Packers). But even though they've only been in the league since 1995, Jacksonville's team, the Jaguars, has made a big mark on the NFL.

When the NFL announced that it was expanding, many cities tried to earn one of the teams. In 1993, Jacksonville was awarded one of the expansion teams, with local businessman Wayne Weaver as the owner. Weaver had two years to get his team ready for its first game, and the first thing he did was hire a coach. Tom Coughlin had been a success at Boston College. Now he was given free rein to create an NFL team from scratch. The NFL gave Jacksonville extra draft picks and allowed the team to choose some players from existing teams. Still, few people expected the Jags to be very good any time soon. It can take years to build a quality NFL team. Coughlin and Weaver were in a hurry, however.

Their quarterback was lefty Mark Brunell, who

combined laserlike accuracy with great **scrambling** ability. His receivers, Jimmy Smith and Keenan McCardell, would become Pro Bowl players. Brunell helped the Jags win their first-ever game in the fifth week of the first season. They won three more and finished their initial campaign at 4–12. In the draft, they solidified their defense with linebacker Kevin Hardy. They also chose superb offensive tackle Tony Boselli to help protect Brunell.

Jaguars' owner Wayne Weaver became a millionaire with a successful women's shoe business.

Tom Coughlin was picked to be the first coach of the new Jaguars.

Seven years after the expansion Jaguars made Tony Boselli the first draft pick in franchise history, the expansion Texans made him the first pick in the 2002 player allocation draft.

The 1996 season, only Jacksonville's second, would prove to be a Cinderella story . . . and the beginning of good times down South. The Jaguars were 8–7 going into the final game of the season. If they beat Atlanta in that game, they would earn a wild-card playoff spot. However, the Falcons, trailing by one point, drove to near the Jags' goal line for a short field-goal try. Atlanta's kicker, Morten

Mark Brunell celebrates after the Jags upset the Broncos in 1996.

Andersen, was one of the NFL's all-time best. He had not missed a kick inside 30 yards all season. Guess what? He **shanked** this one, and the Jaguars were suddenly, surprisingly, in the playoffs at the tender NFL age of two.

The surprises just kept coming. The Jags traveled to Buffalo, where the hometown Bills had never lost a playoff game. Jacksonville battled all game long, and the score was tied at 27–27 late in the game. Then Jacksonville recovered a Buffalo fumble! Jags kicker Mike Hollis nailed a 45-yard field goal, and the baby Jags had won the game!

They could only celebrate briefly, however, for up next were the powerful Denver Broncos. Denver had posted an AFC-best 13–3 record. Their star quarterback John Elway was on his way to a Hall of Fame career. However, the Jaguar defense kept Elway bottled up for most of the game. In the fourth quarter, Brunell led a key touchdown drive, twice scrambling for key first downs. They needed the 10-point lead it created, because Elway and Denver scored again. But the Broncos needed more than that and couldn't get it. Once again, the Cinderella team was a winner by a 30–27 score.

Jaguars' home stadium, ALLTEL Stadium, will play host to Super Bowl XXXIX in January 2005.

Jacksonville held a naming contest in 1991, two years before the city was awarded the franchise. Following Jaguars in the vote were Sharks, Stingrays, and Panthers.

Steve Beuerlein was the Jaguars' original starting quarterback in 1995, but Mark Brunell soon took over and became entrenched in the lineup.

Though they lost in the AFC Championship Game to New England, it was a monumental start for a young team. No other expansion team had ever played for a conference title so quickly. (Second-year Carolina also played for the NFC title the same year.)

Things just kept getting better. Jacksonville's high-scoring offense kept rolling, and the team posted 11 wins in each of the next two seasons. In 1998, they were helped by rookie running back Fred

Jimmy Smith (No. 82) is one of the NFL's top wide receivers.

Fred Taylor combines great speed with power
to bust through the line.

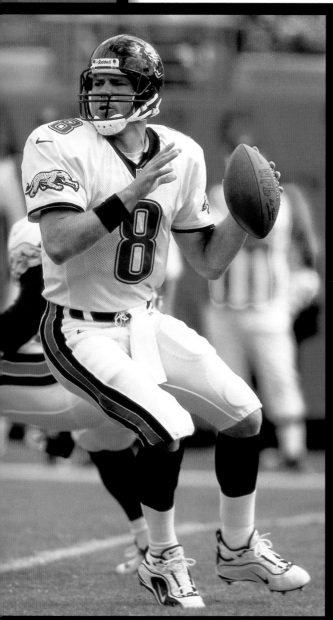

Mark Brunell is one of the best left-handed passers ever.

Taylor, who gave Brunell a new weapon. Taylor ran for 1,223 yards and scored 17 touchdowns.

Taylor and Brunell led the Jaguars to the best record in the entire NFL in 1999 at 14–2. Their offense scored the second-most points in the conference, while their defense gave up the fewest. In a divisional playoff game against Miami, Jacksonville exploded for 62 points. It was the second most points scored in a playoff game in NFL history. The only topper was

Fred Taylor bursts past a Miami defender on his way to a record run in 1999.

the 73 points scored in a 1940 game by the Chicago Bears. The 55-point victory margin (Miami scored 7 points) was the second-most ever, too. It was the most points any Miami team had ever given up in one game. The game's highlight play was Taylor's 90-yard touchdown run, the longest scoring run in playoff history.

Unfortunately, Jacksonville should have saved some of those points for the AFC Championship

Including playoffs, Jacksonville was 15–3 in 1999—0–3 against the Titans and 15–0 against the rest of the league.

Tom Coughlin coached the Jaguars for their first eight seasons before former NFL linebacker Jack Del Rio took over in 2003.

Game. There they lost to the Tennessee Titans 33–14. Cinderella suddenly saw her ride to the Super Bowl turn into a pumpkin.

Though the loss of some key players has led to down years for Jacksonville recently, they're sure to bounce back. After all, Cinderella ended up marrying her prince eventually, right?

Jaguars defenders couldn't catch the Titans' Derrick Mason in the 1999 AFC title game.

CHAPTER FOUR

THE TENNESSEE TITANS

T he team that is today called the Tennessee Titans has gone through three separate lives in pro football—four, if you count a brief stop in Memphis. First, they were part of the old American Football League (AFL). Then they were part of the NFL. Then they moved to Tennessee and got a new name. Through it all, only one man has owned the franchise.

Bud Adams was one of several businessmen who started a new pro football league in 1960 to rival the established NFL. The AFL started with eight teams, including Adams's Houston Oilers. Led by quarterback George Blanda, Houston won AFL titles in 1960 and 1961. Blanda would later become famous as the NFL's "old man," playing until he was 48 years old.

The next big news in Oilers history came in 1968, when they moved into the Houston Astrodome. The enormous indoor stadium was called "the eighth wonder of the world." The Oilers were the

gle-season total ever, 1,934 yards. But once more,
the Oilers fell in the playoffs.

The 1980s were a lost cause for Houston until
the team signed quarterback Warren Moon. With
his slingshot arm and a powerful defense, the
Oilers were the only NFL team to make the playoffs
every year from 1987 to 1993. However, in each of
those seasons, they fell short of their ultimate goal,
the Super Bowl. The worst playoff loss came in
1992. Ahead of Buffalo 35–3 in the second half,
they allowed the Bills to tie the game. It was the
greatest comeback in NFL history, and Houston
lost the game in overtime.

The Oilers bounced back to go 12–4 in 1993, but
another playoff loss was a bitter one. Moon left the
team in the off-season, along with several defensive
stars. In 1994, the Oilers were 2–14, marking the
worst single-season turnaround in league history.

In 1996, Adams tried something new to shake
the team up. The Astrodome was an aging stadium,
and people were not coming out as they had in years
past. He announced he was moving the team to
Tennessee in 1997. It was an odd period for the
team. In 1996, they were the Houston Oilers. In

Warren Moon was one of the NFL's most accomplished passers ever.

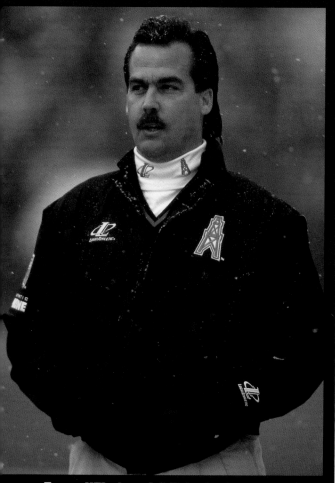

Former NFL player Jeff Fisher has become one of the league's top coaches.

1997, they were the Tennessee Oilers and played in the Liberty Bowl in Memphis. In 1998, still the Oilers, they played in Nashville's Vanderbilt University Stadium. In 1999, they became the Tennessee Titans and played in brand-new Adelphia Coliseum, also in Nashville.

The new digs suited them just fine, and years of playoff frustration came to an end in 1999. Head coach Jeff Fisher had slowly built a championship team. Quarterback Steve McNair and running back Eddie George keyed the offense. The team's 13–3 record was a franchise-best and good for a wild-card spot. In the playoffs, they defeated the Bills, Colts,

Steve McNair is one of the best running quarterbacks ever.

and Jaguars to earn a spot in Super Bowl XXXIV. For
the first time since winning the AFL crown 38 years
earlier, Bud Adams's team would play for a title.

The Titans played the St. Louis Rams in the
championship game. Most gave Tennessee little
chance. The Rams had lit up scoreboards around
the league that season, leading the league with 526
points. However, the Titans gave the Rams all they

Offensive lineman
Bruce Matthews, who
was with the franchise
from 1983 to 2001,
played in more games
(296) than any other
non-kicker in NFL
history.

Eddie George put on a courageous performance in Super Bowl XXXIV.

The franchise avenged its 1992 playoff loss to the Bills with the "Music City Miracle" in 1999: a cross-field lateral on a kickoff return that produced the winning touchdown in the final seconds.

could handle. With just over two minutes left, Tennessee capped a rally from a 16–0 deficit to tie the score at 16–16 on an Al Del Greco field goal.

The Rams stunned the Titans with a 73-yard bomb from Kurt Warner to Isaac Bruce to take the lead. McNair had less than two minutes to try to match Warner, and he nearly made it. The key play of the final drive came when McNair barely avoided being **sacked** and rifled a 16-yard pass to the Rams' 10-yard line. There were just six seconds left and time for one more play.

With almost four decades of frustration hanging on the line, McNair zipped a pass to Kevin Dyson at the five. It seemed as if he would go in to score.

But Rams linebacker Mike Jones made one of the best plays in Super Bowl history. He wrapped up the speedy receiver and tackled him inside the one-yard line. The game ended with the Titans inches away from a tying score.

The team that once was the Oilers and is now the Titans certainly has the talent to leap those final inches in the years to come. Adams is just hoping it doesn't take them another 38 years to give it a shot!

After losing four of five games to start the 2002 season, the Titans won 11 of 12 (including playoffs) before falling to Oakland in the AFC title game.

So close—The Titans were this close to tying Super Bowl XXXIV on the game's final play.

STAT STUFF

TEAM RECORDS

Team	All-time Record	NFL Titles (Most Recent)	Number of Times in Playoffs	Top Coach (Wins)
HOUSTON	4-12-0	0	0	Dom Capers (4)
INDIANAPOLIS	352-367-7	3 (1970)	16	Don Shula (73)
JACKSONVILLE	68-60-0	0	4	Tom Coughlin (72)
TENNESSEE	311-327-6	2* (1961)	17	Jeff Fisher (80)

(* AFL championships)

The Titans (right) and Jaguars are fierce AFC South rivals.

MEMBERS OF THE PRO FOOTBALL HALL OF FAME

HOUSTON

None

JACKSONVILLE

None

INDIANAPOLIS

Player	Position	Date Inducted
Raymond Berry	End	1973
Eric Dickerson	Running Back	1999
Art Donovan	Defensive Tackle	1968
Weeb Ewbank	Coach	1978
Ted Hendricks	Linebacker	1990
John Mackey	Tight End	1992
Gino Marchetti	Defensive End	1972
Leonard (Lenny) Moore	Flanker/Running Back	1975
Jim Parker	Guard/Tackle	1973
Joe Perry	Fullback	1969
Don Shula	Coach	1997
Johnny Unitas	Quarterback	1979

TENNESSEE

Player	Position	Date Inducted
George Blanda	Quarterback/Kicker	1981
Earl Campbell	Running Back	1991
Dave Casper	Tight End	2002
Sid Gillman	Coach	1993
Ken Houston	Strong Safety	1986
John Henry Johnson	Running Back	1987
Charlie Joiner	Wide Receiver	1996
Mike Munchak	Tight End	2001

STAT STUFF

AFC SOUTH CAREER LEADERS (THROUGH 2002)

HOUSTON

Category	Name (Years with Team)	Total
Rushing yards	Jonathan Wells (2002)	529
Passing yards	David Carr (2002)	2,592
Touchdown passes	David Carr (2002)	9
Receptions	Billy Miller (2002)	51
Touchdowns	Corey Bradford (2002)	6
Scoring	Kris Brown (2002)	71

JACKSONVILLE

Category	Name (Years with Team)	Total
Rushing yards	Fred Taylor (1998–2002)	4,784
Passing yards	Mark Brunell (1995–2002)	24,904
Touchdown passes	Mark Brunell (1995–2002)	142
Receptions	Jimmy Smith (1995–2002)	664
Touchdowns	Jimmy Smith (1995–2002)	53
Scoring	Mike Hollis (1995–2001)	764

INDIANAPOLIS

Category	Name (Years with Team)	Total
Rushing yards	Lydell Mitchell (1972–77)	5,487
Passing yards	Johnny Unitas (1956–1972)	39,768
Touchdown passes	Johnny Unitas (1956–1972)	287
Receptions	Raymond Berry (1955–1967)	631
Touchdowns	Lenny Moore (1956–1967)	113
Scoring	Dean Biasucci (1984, 1986–1994)	783

TENNESSEE

Category	Name (Years with Team)	Total
Rushing yards	Eddie George (1996–2002)	8,978
Passing yards	Warren Moon (1984–1993)	33,685
Touchdown passes	Warren Moon (1984–1993)	196
Receptions	Ernest Givins (1986–1994)	542
Touchdowns	Earl Campbell (1978–1984)	73
Scoring	Al Del Greco (1991–2000)	1,060

GLOSSARY

associates—people you work with

budget—an amount of money designated for a specific use

draft—the selection of players by a sports team

era—a period of time known for a particular event or person

expansion—in the NFL, the term used for a new team added to the league

favored—in sports, this describes a team that most people think will win a game

rival—an important or regular opponent

sacked—when a quarterback is tackled behind the line of scrimmage

scrambling—when a quarterback runs out of the pocket and carries the ball downfield or avoids tacklers to make a pass

shanked—to have missed a target very badly, often far from where it was intended

sudden-death overtime—when an NFL game is tied, an extra period is played during which any score by either team wins the game

wild-card—term for playoff teams who have the best records but do not win division titles

TIME LINE

1950 Baltimore Colts join the NFL

1958 Colts win NFL championship

1959 Colts repeat as NFL champions

1960 Houston Oilers founded as part of the AFL (they moved to Tennessee in 1997); win AFL championship

1961 Oilers repeat as AFL champs

1968 Colts win NFL title, but lose to AFL champion New York Jets in Super Bowl III

1971 Colts win Super Bowl V following 1970 season

1984 Colts move from Baltimore to Indianapolis

1995 Jacksonville Jaguars begin play in AFC

1995 Colts reach AFC Championship Game, lose to Steelers

1996 Jaguars advance to AFC Championship Game, quickest trip ever for an expansion team; they lose to New England

1997 Houston Oilers move to Tennessee and in 1999 become the Titans

1999 Jaguars return to AFC title game, but lose again, this time to the Titans

2002 Houston Texans begin play in AFC South

FOR MORE INFORMATION ABOUT THE AFC SOUTH AND THE NFL

BOOKS

Buckley, James Jr., and Jerry Rice. *America's Greatest Game.* New York: Hyperion
Books for Children, 1998.

Buckley, James Jr. *Eyewitness: Football.* New York: DK Publishing, 1999.

Marini, Matt. *Football Top 10.* New York: DK Publishing, 2002.

ON THE WEB

Visit our home page for lots of links about the AFC South:

http://www.childsworld.com/links.html

Note to Parents, Teachers, and Librarians: We routinely verify our Web links to
make sure they are safe, active sites—so encourage your readers to check them out!

INDEX

ABOUT THE AUTHOR

James Buckley Jr. has written more than 35 books on sports for young readers, including *Eyewitness Football* and *America's Greatest Game*, about NFL history. He was an editor at NFL Publishing and contributed to the league's magazines and the Super Bowl Program.